How To Make Cash From Your Crafts

S. Denise Hoyle, MBA

CONTENTS

1 INTRODUCTION

The dictionary says craft means "a special skill, art, or dexterity" or "an occupation requiring special skill, especially any of the manual arts."

Actually, a "craft" can be any hobby you may have – sewing, macramé, needlepoint, cross stitch, embroidery (by hand or machine), knitting, crocheting, woodworking, candle making, soap making, painting, quilting, making dolls, monogramming, silk flower arranging, corn husk art, tapestry – the list goes on and on. Everybody can do something!

Crafts are a modern day remedy for stress. When times are tough, the tough start quilting, cross-stitching, woodworking and more. And crafting is for everybody – men, women, children, elderly and disabled, anyone can turn to crafting for stress relief and as a relaxing hobby.

As more and more people are turning to crafts as a part time "hobby", it is understandable when these people also begin to acquire a "collection" of whatever craft hobby they enjoy. This is where the hobby can take a turn into being a viable part time business. Thousands of men and women are making extra spending money from the crafts they make, and are making the transition from doing their crafts as a hobby to using their craft as a part time or full time business.

It is the business side of your crafts that we will deal with throughout this book. It is our intention to familiarize you with ways to start up your business, how to market your crafts, give you guidelines on how much to charge for your crafts, how and where to advertise, and so on.

2 MAKING CASH FROM YOUR CRAFTS

You can easily make $2,000 or more per month by turning your favorite craft hobby into a business. Spend as much or as little time as you want - work the hours you want! Take a day off whenever you choose! YOU are the boss; this is YOUR business. You can start off small, just working evenings and weekends or get aggressive and turn crafting into a full time, very lucrative business – the choice is yours. A craft business can be started with very little money up front. Simply informing friends and family that you're going to start selling your craft items can help you to get your business started. Have a flyer made up announcing your new business and tack it up on bulletin boards at local grocery stores and other businesses to let people know about the crafts you have for sale. Have business cards printed that can be handed out (see our resources section to find out where to get free business cards). Take pictures of your creations to put into an album to show prospective customers what you have available. Make a mini display in your home "office" that people will see when they come in. Virtually anyone can succeed in this business if they are willing to put genuine effort into it. The market for craft items has never been stronger than it is today!

Even when there seems to be little money for luxuries, people still need gift items for birthdays, anniversaries, graduation, baby showers, Mother's Day, Father's Day, Christmas, Valentine's Day, job promotions, and many other occasions. If your craft item can be personalized, the sales potential increases even more.

People continue to buy decorative crafts and accessories because people are spending more and more time at home and these items satisfy a personal desire to decorate their space and own something beautiful.

Even if you don't have a craft hobby right now - library books and magazines are full of ideas for projects and items that you could make and sell. You need to be aware, however, that not everything you might make will be an instant success. There may be something you create that doesn't turn out to be a very popular item, but on the other hand, you will never know what will succeed if you don't try it. EVERYONE who is, or ever has been, in the craft business will tell you of their fast selling and poor selling items. The trick is to eliminate the poor sellers and keep trying different items – you WILL hit upon some that will be hot sellers.

But, you ask, can a person make a living selling their crafts? The answer is a resounding YES!! A person dealing in crafts who approaches their work in a serious and businesslike manner will do very well. Once the basics are learned you can easily make up to $20,000 a year working part time and from $20,000 to $50,000 or more a year working full time.

The quality of your crafts will determine how successful your business will be. You must make the decision to produce the finest work you possibly can. In addition to being able to make a good living with your crafts, you will also gain a deep sense of self-satisfaction knowing that you are giving your customers products that are well made and will withstand the test of time. Remember, if other people can succeed in a crafts business, YOU CAN TOO!

This portion of "How To Make CASH From Your Crafts" contains detailed information on how to start up your business, how to market yourself, pricing guidelines, information on bookkeeping, taxes, advertising and much more.

The old saying "You are what you think you are" is definitely true. If you have confidence in yourself (and if you don't, you need to start giving yourself some pep talks) and keep an optimistic attitude and outlook on the business and life in general, you will find that the sky is the limit. Train yourself, beginning right now, to think more positively about what you are able to do, tell yourself that nothing is going to stop you from reaching your goals (by the way – have you made some goals?) and believe in yourself and what you are doing. You will be a success in this business!

3 MAKING YOUR CRAFTS

If you are thinking about the possibilities of what to make
and sell (or even if you already have items you're making)
you need to ask yourself a few questions:

- What type of items are you going to make and
  sell in your business? (name them
  specifically.)
- Are you going to make the items yourself or is
  someone going to help you? (husband, wife, a
  son or daughter, friend?)
- How much time can you devote to making
  the items you want to sell? (in order to sell
  them, they have to be made ahead of time,
  unless you have items where you can show
  one and take orders for them – even then they
  have to be made sometime.)
- Is your craft item easy to carry and move – is
  it an item that would be easy to mail if you
  choose to market online or by mail order?
- Is your craft item finished and ready to use?
  Nobody wants to go home and have to finish
  painting an object or figure out how to hang

7

something. (The obvious exception here is if ALL your crafts are the type that the customer would take home to paint or embellish themselves.)

- Is your craft item something that would make a nice gift? Can it be given to anybody – a boy's item to any boy; a woman's item to any woman – in other words it shouldn't have to be custom made or custom fitted. (Custom made or custom fitted items are unique in themselves and are a superior idea if you're only working out of your house, as this type of product could not easily be promoted at a craft show or flea market, where "quantity" sales are important for profit.)

- Is your craft item a "one of a kind" item? The customer will be more likely to buy from you "now" if she knows she cannot readily find the same item at a downtown store tomorrow or next week.

- Where do you want to sell the items? (flea markets, bazaars, at craft shows, through mail order advertising, online – we'll talk more about those things later).

- What distance from your home would be a reasonable distance to travel to craft shows, if you decide to market your crafts by this method?.

Whatever it is that you finally decide upon to make and sell – you MUST have it nicely packaged. In the first place, articles that are not packaged are much more likely to get broken and damaged. An item in a nice package with a printed label attached to it will sell quicker than items that look like they came from the closet or toy box or are laid out like you're running a rummage sale! In addition, customers will want to handle and "try" the items that are lying on the table, but will want to buy one that has not been "used" by every other customer, or that they feel has been handled by many.

The printed label will need to have written on it what the item is, and, if necessary, instructions on how to use the item – you also MUST have your name and address on the label so the customer can order other things from you, or more of the same item that they bought. We also suggest that your name and address be placed ON each item if possible – perhaps in a corner, or the underside in an inconspicuous place, as the package and label will probably be thrown away after the item is taken out of the package.

There is literally NO LIMIT to the ideas for possible items to make! You could come up with new ideas for items or make a variation of an old idea. Check craft books, how-to books, trendy women's magazines and your local library for ideas for items to make. It has been said, "the person who does not read books has no advantage over the person who can't read them". In any home-based business, this is an absolute truth!! You must keep up with changing trends, new ideas and possibilities to make your business even better than before! Look at the following listing of ideas for crafts and see what might appeal to you:

- Artwork (painting, sculpture, wood burning, etc.)
- Baskets
- Batik
- Birdfeeders and birdhouses
- Briefcases
- Books (how-to-books, craft books, calendars, cook-books, books of poems)
- Calligraphy
- Candles

- Cartoons
- Carvings
- Ceramics
- Clocks
- Clothing
- Cross-stitch
- Crochet
- Decor items (wall hangings, centerpieces, lamps, quilts, rugs,)
- Dolls
- Doorknockers
- Dough art
- Dried flowers
- Silk flowers and flower arrangements
- Engravings
- Enameling
- Graphic art (wall decor, note cards, stationery)
- Greeting cards
- Hats
- Household items (lamps, cutting boards, knife racks)
- Ironwork
- Indian crafts
- Jewelry
- Kites

- Knitting
- Knives
- Lamps
- Lathe work
- Leatherwork
- Masks
- Metal sculpture
- Miniatures
- Note cards and stationary
- Paintings
- Papier-mâché
- Photography
- Picture frames
- Plastic canvas
- Posters
- Pottery
- Puppets
- Purses
- Puzzles
- Quilts
- Rugs
- Refrigerator magnets (dough art, wood cutouts, fabric)
- Sewing crafts
- Signs

- Stained glass
- Stuffed toys
- Tatting
- Tole painting
- Toys
- Whistles
- Wind chimes

  Woodworking

The list could go on and on – and somewhere within that list are things that YOU can make! Wherever your interest may lie, you already have some talent, so it will be up to you to bring that talent to life. You will be amazed at what you can do if you just put in the initial effort and each day do something to add fuel to the spark of craft "fire" you've created.

When making a determination of what types of craft items to make, it would be a good thing to remember that craft items priced below $20 will sell the best in many markets. Of course more expensive items will sell also, but you just won't have as many sales as you would if the product was less expensive. It might be a good idea to offer the customer items in different price categories – perhaps you could make a fancy "Cadillac" version as well as a "Chevrolet" version with fewer frills.

Whatever you've decided upon, you should be sure to keep your product line limited to a collection of items with the same common theme. For example, if you are into wind chimes – make a variety of wind chimes – this way you will have a wider variety that will appeal to more people. In other words, making fifty sets of the same wind chime will make you far less money than if you have ten sets of five different styles and types of wind chimes. Not only do different people's tastes vary, but there is also the potential of a customer buying two or three different wind chimes if you have several different styles available.

Don't try to do it all by having wind chimes, dolls, paintings, cross-stitch, ceramics and assorted non-related items in your display. This will tend to confuse the customer and will make it harder to up sell other matching or complementary items. Additionally, trying to create too many things can cause you to spread your time so thin trying to make a large variety of items that you may not be able to do justice to any of them, not to mention the amount of money you'll be spending to get basic supplies for each type of craft. You're much better off to stick with one or two related craft lines and spend your time and money promoting those products.

Keep track of how well your items are selling and which ones are selling the best. If one of your wind chimes is selling like hot cakes, you'll know you need to increase your inventory of them. On the other hand, if one type of wind chime just sits and doesn't get much interest, you know you should discontinue that particular style and put a different type in its place – don't waste space on a dud – try something else.

Even when you limit yourself to wind chimes, for example, don't think you have to try to make EVERY conceivable type of wind chime possible. Just try to have a nice assortment – maybe 8 to 12 different kinds. If you try to have DOZENS of styles, it then becomes a chore for the customer to make a decision of which to buy. If you give a customer too many choices, it makes it easier for him to walk away without deciding on anything.

And, don't forget the most important item – QUALITY! It is the quality of your work that will increase your sales and make repeat sales. If a customer is thrilled with what they have purchased from you, they will more than likely buy another of your products for a friend or relative as a gift. "Word of mouth" advertising and referrals can literally become the lifeblood of your business as satisfied customers recommend your products to their friends.

4 THE CRAFT MARKET

The craft market is a wide-open field. There has never been a better time to start this type of business than right now. As previously stated, the craft market is still a moneymaker regardless of economic conditions. People are always looking for gifts for Mother's Day, Father's Day, graduation, congratulations gifts, house warming gifts, and so on.

So, now you have lots of ideas for products to make and sell, and maybe you already have a good number of items made and ready to sell. The big question is "where do I sell my craft items?"

Of course the first group of people to turn to would be your friends, neighbors, relatives, and people at work. These people have probably all admired the work you do and wish they could make those things – just let them know you are now going to go into business with your crafts and that they are available for them to buy. Ask them to help you get the word out.

CRAFT FAIRS/CRAFT SHOWS

Do some checking in your own local town or county for any craft fairs, bazaars, and flea markets that are held on an annual or periodical basis. Usually most shopping malls will have craft shows sometime in the fall before Christmas and you can rent a space or a table in that craft show. If you have several malls in your area, check with all of them for dates and times of their craft shows and you may find your weekend dates filling up with shows.

Don't limit yourself to just your town – check into what's available in the next county. Maybe you could do a span of several counties. Depending on the time you have available to travel to the craft shows, you may be able to contact a state agency to see what's available throughout the state. In the Resources section at the back of this book we have listed state agencies you can contact as well as craft show promoters from across the nation. If you have friends or relatives in another state and intend to visit them sometime this year you might want to check out any craft fairs for that particular area and schedule your family visit at the same time as the craft fair. This is a great way to save on expenses, plus you'll get to write off a portion of your travel expenses.

Craft fairs and craft shows can be a great source of "instant" money. As soon as you have an ample supply of your craft items made up you can go ahead and schedule yourself to sell at a craft fair. Not only will you be able to make money right away, but also because there are so many craft fair opportunities throughout the year, you can schedule as many as you like. This means that the "beginner" at the craft business can earn a living if they apply themselves.

Although you may be a little nervous before the first few craft shows, you should realize that whatever money you make will be more than if you didn't participate in the show at all! An important thing to remember is to be PREPARED. This means having an ample supply of your craft items on hand so you won't run out the first day. Just consider the craft shows and craft fairs as "paydays", and you'll be so excited you won't be able to contain yourself!

At any craft fair you must have everything you need to

set up your space, and be ready to set it up EARLY! Each fair or show will tell you in advance exactly what they will provide (tables and table coverings, chairs, carpeting, draping for the back and sides of the space, electrical outlets, if you need them, etc). Usually you will just come in and set up your craft items and be ready for the customers, although at some venues you may have to bring your own table, tablecloth and chairs. We suggest that you set up your display on your dining room table ahead of time so you'll have time to rearrange the display if necessary and look it over to see what if anything might be missing – signs, displays, etc.

If you get to the show early and get set up quickly, you'll probably have time to walk around and see what else is being offered there and perhaps talk to a few of the other show participants. This is always a good time to check out the competition, make notes on their pricing, and be on the lookout for new craft ideas that you may be able to use or improve. Be sure to be back at your space before the doors open up or people arrive – you won't want to miss any of the early shoppers! Another tip is to try and get a spouse, friend or someone else you trust to attend the show with you so you can take food or bathroom breaks without leaving your table unattended. If it's not possible to bring someone with you for the whole show, see if they can maybe stop by for a "lunch hour" or try making friends with the show participants surrounding your table and offer to take turns watching each other's tables if the need arises.

Since you have taken the trouble to attend the show, you'll want to be able to make the most of what it has to offer. Stay at your booth as much as possible, talk to the customers, let them "play" with one of your toys, or touch one of your craft items to inspect the quality of it. Watch how the customers interact with your items and listen for any comments – positive or negative – that they might make about your crafts. Also make note of any special requests, if you can't oblige them now you may want to think about taking custom orders.

The "secret" to selling your products is by generating excitement and enthusiasm about them. After all, you made them, and you surely must be proud of your handiwork, so don't be afraid to show your enthusiasm as you show your crafts. You know that you are offering customers a high-quality product and one that they will be proud to use or give as a gift. Your enthusiasm and excitement becomes contagious and soon customers are bringing their friends to your booth, and they often will have them pre-sold on your craft items. Remember that an enthusiastic salesperson with a mediocre product can easily outsell a reserved, quiet salesperson with a good product, so what do you think enthusiasm will do for your high quality products?

If you have craft items that can be easily demonstrated you will be able to attract crowds to your booth. Playing with the toys or demonstrating how a craft works attracts much more attention and interest than if the items are merely lying motionless on the table. Demonstrations result in sales. Time also passes much more quickly if you are busy demonstrating your products than if you're just sitting and watching the clock.

After you've made a sale be sure to thank the customer for his purchase. At the same time assure the customer that he will be happy with the purchase and by all means make it easy for the customer to buy more of the product later by providing him with information about how to place a mail, Internet or telephone order. If you have small catalogs or flyers you'll want to hand them out to the customers as well as to people that are just "looking", as they may see something they like and come back later to make the purchase.

Occasionally you will have someone try to talk you into taking less than your listed price for an item. This usually happens more on the last day of the show when someone will come up and say something like "I know you don't want to lug this home, so I'll give you _____ (always much less than what your price is). We simply respond by thanking them for the offer, but since this is what we do for a living, we know that our regular price is fair, and that it has no expiration date on it, therefore will not "spoil" before the next craft show. We also show that customer our catalog and let them know that it will be more expensive if they order it through the mail because they'll have to pay shipping on it, so it would really be to their advantage to go ahead and purchase it right here at the show.

SHOPPING MALL CRAFT SHOWS

Throughout the Christmas season various malls will have craft shows in the walkways and areas between the stores. These will usually be a Thursday through Sunday, or sometimes only a Saturday and Sunday. They are typically not very expensive to get into, and are a great way to get your crafts out to the public. Of course, a lot of the people who come by to browse are not necessarily coming to the mall for a craft show, as they would be if it were specifically a craft show set up at a civic center or the like. However, these people are also doing their shopping for Christmas, and they might as well be buying your craft items on their way into other stores to make purchases.

SELLING THROUGII THE MAIL

Another avenue for you to explore for selling your products is through mail order. There are advantages and disadvantages to selling via mail order. An advantage is that you don't have to have a big supply of products on hand like you do for craft fairs and bazaars, etc. – you can make them up as you need them for orders. In addition, you can work right out of your home and not have to drive anywhere to make a sale or show your crafts.

The main disadvantage to mail order advertising (magazines, etc.) is that the "lead" time (the time between when you have to pay for your ad and when it actually gets to people) for advertising could be several months before the magazine gets to the people you want to read it. There is one magazine that we advertise in, for example, where the deadline for the **March/April** issue is **November 15**! This means that you have spent your advertising money by November 15 and won't see **any** results back from it until around the middle of February when the magazine goes out to the general public.

I'm not saying you should not do magazine advertising – we do it ourselves – but you have to be aware of the fact that you will have to wait for the results of this type of advertising.

If you do go with magazine advertising, we highly suggest you try some classified advertising before you pay the more expensive rates for display advertising. (More about advertising in the section on advertising).

You might like to make up a leaflet on the items you have available, showing a picture or line drawing of the items along with a description of the item, and, of course, the price of the item and ordering information giving your name and address, etc. These little flyers or leaflets could then be handed out to people, or you could get a mailing list and mail the leaflets to the individuals on the mailing list.

If you want to try this type of advertising, there are a couple ways The U S Postal Service has a service called "Every Day Direct Mail" that is a PERFECT way to start advertising your business. Go to their website: https://www.usps.com/business/every-door-direct-mail.htm and get all the information. In a nutshell, Every Door Direct Mail service is an easy, cost-effective way to reach potential customers near your business. Just create your mail pieces however you like, then select postal routes and pay for postage online, or you can pay for it at your post office. Next, take your mailing to your local Post Office™ for delivery to every household on your chosen routes. Using the online mapping tool you can choose among postal routes based on the demographics you choose, (whether you're wanting to select residential areas for your service, or business neighborhoods for your new website development business, etc) then the postal service delivers to every address on your selected routes. There is no permit fee to pay for and at this printing the fee is a mere 18.3 cents per mailing piece! There is no minimum number of mailing pieces you must reach, but there is a maximum of 5,000 per day for using Every Door Direct Mail.

If your business is "national", rather than your "local neighborhood", and you have names and addresses of customers throughout the country, OR if you're getting a mailing list to send out information, you will need to go to your local Post Office and make arrangements to get a bulk mail permit. At the time of this printing, the permit will cost you an initial one-time fee of $225.00, and you'll have to pay the annual fee of around $225.00. The one-time fee is, of course, paid only once when you set up the bulk mailing account. The annual fee is, naturally, paid every year, and the year runs from January 1 through December 31. So, if, around the middle of October you decide you'd like to do this type of advertising, determine how many leaflets or flyers you're going to mail out to see if it would be to your benefit to pay the annual fee at that time, and then have to pay it again in December for the following year.

The good thing about using the bulk mailing is that letters or flyers you send out will cost you, right now, 30.9 cents each, instead of the regular 49 cents, which is the first class rate (these rates are subject to change as postal rates may change).

With the bulk mail you have to send out a minimum of 200 in each mailing (the post office will give you instructions and all the necessary items you'll need to start your mailing), but if you want to get your flyers or brochures out to the public, you'll probably be sending out more than 200 anyway.

Who will you send your leaflets to? You should already have compiled a list of names and addresses of people you have sold items to, so that's a beginning! If you look at any income opportunities type magazine, or even in the magazines you regularly read, you'll find companies that specialize in mailing lists. These companies can get for you any type of mailing list you might need. Maybe you want mail order buyers that have children if your products are toys, or maybe you want a listing of women who sew if your product is quilt patterns, or patterns for toys, etc. The contact person at the mailing list company will be able to give you additional information.

SELLING OVER THE INTERNET

It has become relatively easy over the past several years to take a craft business online. If you don't have the time or energy to setup your own website you can list your items for sale at online auction websites like eBay.com or craft sites like Etsy and others. You could start there if you'd like and then after you make a few sales you should consider registering your own domain name, which shouldn't cost more than $10/year. Buy some web design software and create your own website, or your domain name registrar (we prefer GoDaddy.com but there are numerous reputable firms out there) likely has web templates, available for a small fee, that will help you to have your crafts displayed online very quickly and easily.

Pick and choose from these options to find the ones that will work the best for you. We simply want to impress upon you that "crafting" is a wide-open field and the sooner you get started the sooner the money will come. Why not take that first step today to start a business that could change your future. If you're already "dabbling" in crafts, you literally have nothing to lose and everything to gain.

5 CHARGING FOR YOUR CRAFTS

Now let's get into the actual money end of the craft business. What should I charge for my embroidered wall hanging, or toy, or stuffed animal, or piece of artwork? It is often difficult for beginning crafters to price their work. Usually we'll think back to our high school days and remember the teacher explaining the principle of supply and demand. Perhaps you remember the notion that, as the price is lowered, the demand becomes greater.

Almost all craftspeople start off with prices that are too low. Usually, a person has a lower opinion of his own work than others will who see it. The craftsperson knows the small flaws there may be in the work that would never be noticed by the public. Also, the craftsperson may not have spent a lot of time making the item, so therefore thinks it should be sold dirt-cheap.

These ideas are **wrong, wrong, wrong**!!! You are a professional at what you are doing and you need to be paid a good price for the things you create!

The easiest way to find the right selling price for your products is, first of all, arbitrarily selecting a starting price for your items. Check around for items others have that might be similar in amount of time spent on making the item, or are similar types of products and compare their prices. Be sure to determine the cost of materials plus the cost of your time, and realize that your asking price should be at least two to three times your "cost of goods". Select a "median" type of price as a starting point for your items. Sell the items at this initial price for two or three craft shows or bazaars and keep detailed records of all of your sales. After this, at every **second** craft show, keep raising your prices slightly until you know you have reached the limit in your pricing, then back down a notch to establish your regular retail price.

This experimentation of pricing should be done during the spring and summer months. Experimentation of this type during the Holiday season will give you false results, because if the economy is good virtually anything may sell

at Christmas, regardless of what you are charging.

As you probably already know – you will make the most profit on an item if you sell it yourself – at craft fairs or online. However, if your items are the right type, you could **sub-wholesale** them – that is if it is the kind of item that the boy scouts, for example, could sell as a money maker for their group, you would sub-wholesale the item to them for 50% of what your regular retail price is, and they would turn around and sell it for the regular retail price, keeping the additional money as their profit. In order to do this, you would have to be able to make some profit on your half of the money that you'd receive. You will need to have as accurate as possible the money and time invested into your products for pricing purposes.

While the price of the materials in your products and time invested are very important, they are not to be the sole consideration for making your final price. Like we mentioned before, your retail price should be the highest price the market will bear. After all, whatever you make would be unique and your talent and experience are worth money too!

Keep in mind, however, that a good craft item should

have a low materials cost. Ask yourself if you can make between $15 and $20 an hour producing your item. If you cannot make that much, you need to find a better way to make your item or find a new item to make. Many good craft items can be produced at the rate of $50 to $100 an hour by someone with experience.

You should know that for this type of selling the majority of sales will be **impulsive** and most impulse sales will be less than $20.00. However, don't limit your products to ones that sell for less than $20 – it is a good idea to have a variety of price points as well as a variety of products.

6 STARTING YOUR BUSINESS

There are three types of business organizations that you have to choose from in order to create your business. The three choices are (1) sole proprietorship, (2) partnership and (3) corporation.

The most common type of business organization for home-based businesses is the sole proprietorship. This type of business only has one principal owner who is responsible for any debts that the business may incur and this owner pays taxes on the net income of the business. This type of business is the easiest to start or terminate - and this is the type that we would recommend for you.

The second choice for your business organization is the partnership. In this type of business, two or more individuals agree to co-own a business. The basic problem with the partnership is that any of the partners could make a major decision without the approval or knowledge of the other partner or partners. If this major decision happens to be a bad decision, all of the partners will suffer. If this major bad decision causes the business to fail with mountains of bills left behind all of the partners are equally responsible, not just the one who made the wrong decision. In addition, if there are not enough assets in the business to satisfy the debts, the partners' personal assets could be seized to satisfy the debts to the creditors. If you choose to go with the partnership, be sure to go to a lawyer and get the necessary paperwork drawn up so that each of the partners knows what their rights and responsibilities are.

The third type of business organization is the corporation. A corporation is a business set up by law to act as a single person. There are usually several people involved in setting up the corporation. You would have to go through a lawyer to get the corporation set up, naming a board of directors and officers. The advantage of a corporation is that each person involved is limited financially to the amount of money he has invested in case of a business failure. The disadvantage of a corporation for a small business is that it requires much more paperwork and recordkeeping. Tax returns have to be filed for the corporation as well as individual tax forms for the persons involved, which results in additional time and accounting expense.

We would advise you to keep your business organization and recordkeeping as simple as possible in order that you can spend as much time as possible doing what you really want to do -- make money!! In other words, if you aren't burying yourself with paperwork you can concentrate on building up your business. We'll go into more detail on recordkeeping a little later.

7 NAMING YOUR BUSINESS

Probably one of the first major tasks for you is to pick a name for your new business. Let me advise you against picking a fancy long "catchy" name that may be hard for your customers to remember. It is, after all, your business, and you can name it whatever you want, but let me warn you about the pitfalls of the fancy "hard to remember" name. Unless you list your business name in the yellow pages of the phone book under the proper heading for your type of craft business, your customers will not be able to get hold of you. A general business listing in the phone book white pages with your "catchy" name simply will not work. Your customers may think your business name is "cute" but a few days or weeks later they will not be able to remember it. If you wish to use something like "The Monogram Lady", "Woodworking King", or "Crafty Crafts", be sure to contact your telephone company representative about yellow page advertising.

Just as we advised you to keep your business organization simple – we advise keeping the business name simple also. How about   "Diana's Doll Repair", or "Wally's Wood Works", or "Susie's Sewing". Using your name as part of the business name will be easy for the customer to remember and you won't have to file for a fictitious name.

After deciding on your business name, you'll need to get some business cards made – usually the minimum order is 500 and an estimate for the cost would be around $25 to $30. You can get 250 full color cards for free from VistaPrint, or get 250 for just $14.95 at iPrint. You will want to give out a business card to all of your new customers for repeat business and also for them to refer their friends to you. Again, make the business card simple and to the point with your business name and a logo if you want to have a logo, then your address and phone number at the bottom of the card.

In addition to business cards, you should have some small self-adhesive labels made with your name, address and phone number. Attach one of the labels to every craft item you make (placed in an inconspicuous place) so the customer will have a ready reference to find you when he needs you again. These labels will be permanently attached to the craft items so will not get lost like flyers and business cards sometimes do.

8 BUSINESS LICENSE

Licensing requirements vary from state to state and city-to-city, so you will need to check with your city clerk's office to see what your local requirement is. Some cities or counties require a business license for a home-based business, while others do not. The same thing applies to sales tax – a state requirement. Sales tax will need to be collected if you live in a state that has a state sales tax. You will need to get a resale (tax) number from the state and they will send you the proper forms and instructions for sending the sales tax you've collected back to the state either monthly or quarterly. (See the listing of state government information telephone numbers at the back of this book). Sales tax must be collected on everything you sell retail if your particular state requires sales tax. (If you are mailing craft items to out of state customers, there is generally no tax to be collected on those sales – only within your own state but make sure to check.)

When you purchase materials and supplies be sure to give the suppliers (see listing of wholesale suppliers in the back of this book) your state tax ID number so you won't have to pay sales tax on them at the time of purchase. The state doesn't want to collect tax twice on the same goods (once from you when you buy the materials and the second time from the person you sell the items to). Therefore, when you buy the materials and supplies with no tax, by showing your tax identification number, the clerk or supplier knows you will collect tax when you sell the item to your customer.

Don't let the requirement of collecting sales tax prevent you from going into a craft business. The collection of and turning in sales tax is a very minor, but important, task in this business, and is worth the time it takes to do the paperwork!

9 WORK FROM THE GARAGE OR FIND A BUSINESS LOCATION?

WORK OUT OF YOUR GARAGE!!! This is a "Home Based Business" and you will have advantages that retail outlets don't have.

First of all you can advertise "FREE DELIVERY" and you'll be able to do it because you don't have to sit in your retail establishment all day "waiting" for customers to come in. In addition you can advertise "CRAFTS SHOWN BY APPOINTMENT ONLY" and be able to do it because you don't have to sit in your retail establishment all day "waiting" for customers to come in. You can be the guest of honor at a club meeting and take a selection of your crafts to show to the club members. You'll be able to set up a booth at the fair, or at a craft festival and not have to pay rent on a business location or have to hire employees to run the business while you're out showing your crafts.

You will have all of your craft supplies in one place (your home) instead of lugging some things you want to work on to the "shop" and having supplies in two places. It never fails – what you need is in the place you're not!

You can start your supper while you're working on your crafts. You'll be at home when the kids get off the school bus. Working at home gets better all the time! Don't even think about a business location, especially to start out – stay at home with this business!

10 BOOKKEEPING

Bookkeeping is probably the most important aspect of your new business. You will want to keep accurate records of your expenses and income for tax purposes, and then keep your tax returns and records for a minimum of five years. Although bookkeeping is important, it needn't be scary – it actually isn't hard, just something you need to be conscientious about. If you get into the habit of keeping all of your receipts (postage, bills from printers for printing flyers, business cards, labels, craft supplies, etc.), you will not have a problem at the end of the year when you get ready to file your income taxes. One note here – be sure to keep ALL business related receipts, whether you pay by check or with cash. Even .55-cent postage receipts or a $1.29 tube of paint paid for in cash can add up to many dollars throughout the year! We suggest that you get a manila expandable folder (perhaps one that has 12 compartments marked for the months of the year), make labels for each of the expense categories (postage, telephone bills, advertising, office supplies, etc.) and put the labels on top of the "months" compartments. File every receipt as soon as possible in the proper section then at the end of the year you'll have everything in order.

In addition, it is extremely important that you keep track of your mileage – this could possibly be the single biggest tax write off you have. We suggest that you get a small pocket calendar in which you can keep track of your DAILY trips. For example on Monday the 3rd you may have beginning odometer reading 11,235.6, ending reading 11,247.4 along with a notation "Mary Smith" because you've delivered some crafts to her consignment shop. At the end of the year go back through the calendar and add up each day's mileage to get a grand total for the year. Besides craft supplies, the mileage may be the biggest deduction you will have, and the current IRS deduction of 56 cents per mile can add up to be a big deduction. The pocket calendar then becomes part of your tax records for the year. (See sample pocket calendar pages in back of this book).

You will need to open a separate checking account to keep the business income and expenses separate from your personal expenses. If you will be taking charges for purchases (Visa or MasterCard), you will have to have a business account and let the bank officer opening your account for you know that you want to be able to take Visa and MasterCard and they will fill out the necessary paperwork for you and give you all of the supplies you will need, or will head you in the right direction to make an application that will allow you to take charge cards. There are several companies that offer credit card services that are separate from your bank, so those options are available if your bank will not set you up as a credit card merchant or if you'd prefer to use a company like PayPal or Square to take credit cards (see "Resources" at the back of this book for a listing of these companies).

It has been our experience that nearly all of the crafts will be paid for with cash or check. However, we have discovered that by accepting charge cards, the credit card sales will probably amount to at least 25 to 40 percent of your annual sales. Also you might be able to make additional sales if you do offer to take Visa or MasterCard. Sometimes the potential customer may not have enough cash on hand and will prefer to charge the purchase or might buy several items instead of just one. Other people prefer to charge so they don't have to carry around cash and you might lose these sales if you don't accept credit card purchases.

On the other hand, if you elect to keep your business simple it would not be necessary to offer Visa and MasterCard. If you choose to go the simple and easy route (at least at the beginning – you can always apply for a merchant account later), you will be able to just open a personal checking account with your name, rather than the business name, and have "special account" printed on the checks. This method will eliminate the business charges that you would have if you opened a regular business account.

You will need to get a record book that you can use to keep track of your craft sales (you can keep track of them by day, week, or month – you'll need this information for your sales tax return, as well as for end of the year Federal taxes).

If you prefer you could devise a record-keeping sheet instead of a book where you can record all of the necessary information:

DATE   **Craft Items Sold**   **Price**

You might also want to add a category to put the customer's name and address beside their order (for mailing list purposes) unless you're keeping a separate card or database record on each customer.

We HIGHLY recommend that you either setup a customer database on your computer or keep a separate 3x5 card on EACH CUSTOMER that includes the customer's name, address and phone number. Write the date and a listing of items the customer bought from you. Keep these cards in an alphabetical card file, filing each card by the customer's last name. If that customer buys from you again, simply pull their card out of your file and add the new purchase date and what the customer bought.

If you have a computer it would be advisable to put the names and addresses in a database file so that you can send information to them periodically about new items you have or perhaps a mini-catalog of all your products. The customer may have only bought one or two items from you, which means they like your type of work and probably would have bought more if they could have at the time. By sending flyers and catalogs to your customers, you can literally DOUBLE or TRIPLE your sales throughout the year.

Regardless of what method you want to use for keeping track of your income and expenses, I would recommend that you go to your local Internal Revenue Service office or to IRS.gov and get a "Schedule C" - the form for reporting a profit or loss from a "sole proprietorship" type of business. Look over the form to see how they have the expense categories broken down. By using this as a guideline, you will be more aware of what type of expenses are used for a tax deduction and you will be able to separate your expenses accordingly.

Whether you do your own year-end taxes or have an accountant or bookkeeper do them for you – you'll be ahead of the game if you keep all of your receipts throughout the year. Also, make sure you keep all of your tax returns, records and receipts for a minimum of five years, just in case of an audit.

11 SETTING BUSINESS GOALS

Up to this point we have talked about getting your business off on the right foot. Now we want to talk a little bit about making sure that the business stays on the right path – through goal setting.

It is true that "if you aim at nothing, you will hit it". It is also a fact that if you stood outside your car, put it in gear, and backed off, there's no possible way that the car would stay on the road! By the same token, if you don't set some specific plans and goals for your business – how will you ever know if you're on the right road or if you're heading for the ditch? How will you know if you've accomplished anything at all? Are you moving forward or backward? Are you even moving?

Take some time right now and write down a few goals and then expand on them later. What do you really want to accomplish with your business (some extra grocery money? a little more money to buy a new TV, furniture or help pay college expenses for your child? a part-time work at home job? a full time business?). How much time can you devote to your craft business?

There are other questions you will think of relating to business goals. You should sit down with four sheets of paper for working out your goals – you need to have weekly goals, monthly goals, 1-year goal plan and a 5-year goal plan.

At the beginning your 1 year and 5 year goal planning sheets may be pretty empty, but as you go along, they will fill up. Your immediate attention will be on the weekly and monthly goals. These have to be specific "I will do this first, I will do this second, I will do this third" type of goals. Then each day do something! Your weekly and even monthly goals will be changing and will need to be somewhat flexible, but that does not mean that you will disregard them! As you write and re-write the goal and daily "to do" sheets, and make sure you have accomplished something each day, you'll be amazed at how fast the whole business will come together. After a few weeks, then months, you can look back and see that the simple goal setting details were the very thing that helped you get your business off the ground.

You can keep down a lot of confusion and wasting of time if you'll get a year or 18 month calendar for keeping track of advertisements you have coming out, craft fairs you've scheduled and so on. This will eliminate running the same ad twice or forgetting to run it again, etc. If you later decide not to run that ad or do that mailing you can X through that date and know it would be available for something else.

While we're on the subject of planning your calendar, I want to mention to you about the tremendous potential of the Christmas Season, Mother's Day, Easter and Valentine's Day for your craft business. We'll talk about this again in the section on advertising, but we feel these four times of the year are so very important to the success of your business that it needs to be highlighted here.

You may not be aware of the fact that many retailers do half of their annual business during the Christmas season. What this means to you is that you need to get the word out about your business as often as possible from the first of October through Christmas – attend craft fairs, give out brochures, send out catalogs of products, check with the shopping malls in your area for craft shows they have scheduled.

Your goals could include items like "attend three craft fairs during the fall months", "offer to be a speaker at two club meetings", "mail flyers or catalogs to all the people on my mailing list of customers". Set your goals according to how much time you have to work this business and whether you just want some extra part time spending money, or if your goal is to grow into a full time business.

12 ADVERTISING YOUR SERVICES

How do you get the word out that you are now in a crafts business and have products for the public to buy? Obviously, if you have rented spaces in craft fairs and bazaars, your mere presence will let the people know you have something to sell.

There are several other ways that you can advertise your business. First of all, give out those business cards to friends and family to inform them and also tell them to pass the word along to anyone they know that is in the market for your type of craft items.

Mailing flyers to a local area is an excellent way to get the word out in mass. If you want to try this type of advertising, there are several things you will need to do. First of all, go to your local Post Office and make arrangements to get a bulk mail permit. This permit will cost you an initial one-time fee of around $225, and you'll have to pay the annual fee of around $225. The one-time fee is, of course, paid only once when you set up the bulk mailing account. The annual fee is, naturally, paid every year, and the year runs from January 1 through December 31. So, if, around the middle of October you decide you'd like to do this type of advertising, determine how many leaflets you're going to mail out to see if it would be to your benefit to pay the annual fee at that time, and then have to pay it again in December for the following year.

The good thing about using the bulk mailing process is that letters or flyers you send out will cost you, right now, 30.9 cents each, instead of the regular 49 cents, which is the first class rate (these rates are subject to change as postal rates may change).

With bulk mail you have to send out a minimum of 200 pieces in each mailing (the post office will give you instructions and all the necessary items you'll need to start your mailing), but if you want to get your leaflets out to the public, you'll probably be sending out more than 200 anyway.

One good way of getting the word out to every home in the community would be to call your local post office and find out their procedure for sending out a bulk mailing to every person on a particular mailing route. The U S Postal Service has a service called "Every Day Direct Mail" that is a PERFECT way to start advertising your business. Go to their website: https://www.usps.com/business/every-door-direct-mail.htm and get all the information. In a nutshell, Every Door Direct Mail service is an easy, cost-effective way to reach potential customers near your business. Just create your mail pieces however you like, then select postal routes and pay for postage online, or you can pay for it at your post office. Next, take your mailing to your local Post Office™ for delivery to every household on your chosen routes. Using the online mapping tool you can choose among postal routes based on the demographics you choose, (whether you're wanting to select residential areas for your service or business neighborhoods) then the postal service delivers to every address on your selected routes. There is no permit fee to pay for and at this printing the fee is a mere 18.3 cents per mailing piece! There is no minimum number of mailing pieces you must reach, but there is a maximum of 5,000 per day for using Every Door Direct Mail.

If your products are something that could easily be sold by mail, then you will need to let as many people as possible know that they can order your products from you.

There are two general types of national advertising that you might want to consider – classified advertising and display advertising. Both types of advertising have to be placed in a magazine from 1 to 3 months ahead of when the magazine is actually sent out to the subscribers. For classified advertising you have to be able to "sell" your product in a few words and make the ad appealing enough for the consumer to want to buy your item.

You will need to get copies of various magazines that cater to the type of people who would be in the market for your product – if you make baby toys, you wouldn't want to advertise in a sporting magazine, etc.

Write to each magazine that you've chosen and ask for a "media kit". The media kit will include advertising rates, deadlines for the ads, dates that the magazine comes out to the public and other assorted information such as how big the circulation is, the type of readership the magazine has, etc. Also, they should include a current issue of that particular magazine.

Check the classified ad section of each of the magazines you've selected to see if they have headings that would correspond to the type of item that you are selling. See how those ads are written – read them all and you'll get the feel of how they should be written. Then sit down and write and re-write your classified ad until you're satisfied with the way it sounds. You'll know for sure how it sounds when it comes out in the magazine and you see what the response is to it.

Classified ads are generally short, 15 to 20 words, so you have only a little space to prove to your prospects that your products are going to be useful to them.

Your ad should have catchy phrases in it to catch the

reader's attention -- **just released! NEW!, For the first time**, etc. You need to zero in on the customer's hot buttons. What is good about what you are selling that will make a customer call you? Is it the color, the size, the warranty, the appearance? Tell the customer why **your** item is better. Is yours the most recent, more colorful, cheaper, more reliable, more compact? Is it made of leather and not vinyl, of metal rather than plastic? What will your product do for the customer? Let customers know what sets you apart from the others.

A good mail order ad, whether a classified or display, has four key elements: a) a description of what you are selling, b) a sales pitch, c) a premium incentive, and d) a response vehicle.

a) Description of the item. Suppose you are selling a new educational toy that really is a one of a kind item. You will have to motivate parents of the value of this new toy for their children.

b) The sales pitch. A good sales pitch gets the prospect involved at once. Just as we talked about earlier, use the catchy words. A few persuasive words can motivate people to come to you, if used correctly in the course of your advertisement.

c) Premium incentive. A good classified ad will give the reader a reason to contact you. What can you do for the prospect if he answers your ad immediately? Maybe you have some free gift (a toy whistle, toy car, etc.), free personalization or perhaps a couple of dollars off for new customers.

d) Response vehicle. This is simply a return address, website or phone number to which they may come see you or call you or send their order to you.

A sample ad, as an example, might be one that I run selling my **"How to Make Scarves"** book and my **"50 Wedding Projects"** book. The classified ads go as follows:

HOW TO MAKE SCARVES plus 101 ways to tie

them. This 100-page book goes into detail showing how scarves are the versatile accessory. $9.95 + $2.00 P&H. Denise Hoyle, 4565 Deerfield Dr, Dept BK, Pensacola, FL 32526.

50 WEDDING PROJECTS from veils to bouquets. Make your wedding beautiful, affordably. $9.95 + $2.00 P&H. Denise Hoyle, 4565 Deerfield Dr, Dept BK, Pensacola, FL 32526.

These both get down to the nitty gritty and are to the point – description of item – sales pitch – response vehicle. The only thing missing is the premium incentive, and that apparently has not caused any problem with the ads, because they both are getting very good results.

And, by the way, speaking of good results, you should keep running your classified ad in a magazine as long as you continue to get good results! How do you know if you are making any money with your classified advertising? Good question!

Good records are a MUST regardless of what type of advertising you are doing. We suggest that you make an "Advertising Record Sheet" for each classified ad that you are placing in a magazine (see sample in the Sample Forms section at the back of this book). An advertising record sheet is used for each classified ad that you place, indicating the cost of the ad, date the magazine will come out, etc. Keep these record sheets in a three-ring binder because you will be using them on a daily basis.

When orders come in, you must record the order on the advertising record sheet and record the date, then under the "sales" column put the Daily number of orders, running total of orders, daily cash sales (total amount of dollars brought in that day), and figure the running total of cash sales.

If you are keeping a consistent record on your "Advertising Record Sheet" (and that is the ONLY way you can tell if any ad is profitable or not), you will simply need to add up all your expenses, then subtract the expense amount from the total amount of money you have received from the "total sales to date" (running total) column on the advertising record sheet.

Your expenses will include:

- the cost of the ad.
- the cost of making the product that has been ordered
- the cost of postage to mail out the item to the customer

the cost of packaging materials (padded envelope, box, etc.)

If you take your total earnings and subtract your costs and still have a profit, then your ad is successful. Even if you made only $100 profit on a particular ad keep in mind that you did indeed make a profit, and considering the additional money you can make on follow-up sales, your profit will be even greater! Running such ads in the future will earn you $100 many more times and help to make your business highly profitable.

One side note about classified advertising. Usually small local newspapers will not be very expensive for your classified ads. Or if you have a "Shopper", "Thrifty Nickel", or "Penny Saver" type of paper, you may want to try placing your classified ad there.

It has been our experience that people will usually place one classified ad and if they don't get flooded with phone calls and orders they never advertise again. This is the WRONG attitude! Classified advertising (and advertising in general) is NOT a one-time thing! It is those people who continue to run their ads that get the business. For example, your first ad might not have resulted in a single sale. However, the second or third time the same ad comes out and people keep seeing it, they'll start thinking "This person must be having good results with this ad and must have a thriving business – think I'll go ahead and order some of their products".

We want to caution you, however, that if your ad has

run two or three times and you have not made any profit on it, stop the ad! You must then either re-work the ad to make it more appealing, or use a different craft item to advertise, or advertise in a different magazine or newspaper. Be sure the magazine has the right kind of readership for the product that you are advertising.

Display ads are the big picture ads you see in every magazine and newspaper you pick up. These ads are costly, but vary in price from one periodical to another. Again, write in for a "media kit", which will give you all the information you'll need to know about prices, sizes of ads, deadlines, etc. Look through the magazine to see the way various ads are laid out and what all is said in the display ads. This might be the time you could go for a "coupon" ad – a small display ad in which you would give a discount on the product if they have the "coupon" from the magazine. Or, you could offer a FREE item of some sort when they order the product you are advertising. Or, if you have a "grouping" of several items (5-7 different items), offer the FREE gift for each order of 3 or more products.

To repeat what we said earlier, you would have to have your ad and money in to the magazine probably 1 to 3 months ahead of when it goes out to the subscriber, so this method is not an "overnight" moneymaker.

There is money to be made in both display and classified advertising, but you have to keep accurate records to make sure you are getting enough business to pay for the cost of the ad. If you find an ad that doesn't pay off, you might try re-writing the ad, sometimes just a different choice of words makes all the difference. Trial and error will teach you some big lessons, but at least if you learn from them, you will have accomplished something. We have all had advertisements that have "bombed", as well as those that are a huge success. Just remember, if you <u>never</u> place the first ad, you're absolutely assured of selling NOTHING!

One thing to remember is to always keep track of EVERY individual that orders from you or writes for additional information – you will need these names and addresses to start your own mailing list. You will want to notify these people of any new items you have or send them information once in awhile to remind them of the other products you have available that they may want to order. It is our suggestion that when someone buys something from you, you should send him or her a flyer on other products or a mini-catalog of your products about a month after the purchase. It is a well-known fact that if someone orders from you once, they are the very BEST prospect for additional orders! Plus, it's much cheaper to keep a current customer than to attract a new one.

Keep very close records on your customers, what they are ordering and the dates of each order so you can send "follow-up" information to encourage them to place additional orders from you.

Another item that is very important if you're doing business by mail is that you absolutely MUST enclose information about additional products with EVERY order that you send out. NEVER send out a "naked" order (a "naked" order is one where you'd only put the craft item in a box and mail it out). This would be the biggest mistake you could make! The customer who placed the order will very likely order more of your products, but unless you let them know what they are, they will think all you have is the one item that was ordered. Always include a catalog of products or a flyer of another product. Your "catalog" doesn't have to be a fancy 3-color glossy paged catalog! Line drawings of your products or photographs with typed descriptions of each item put together on regular 8 1/2 x 11" paper will do just as well – you can make black and white copies on color paper or color copies on white paper for a few cents more per page at your local copy shop. You can quite possibly DOUBLE, TRIPLE, or

QUADRUPLE the amount of money you'll make if you will put together some type of catalog or flyers of products and include them with the orders you're sending out!

Other methods of advertising you can use are simply handing out leaflets or flyers to people, tack a flyer to bulletin boards at grocery stores, fabric stores and local convenience stores. Flyers and leaflets are inexpensive to make and the more people you hand them out to the more business you will get.

You can also make a "mini-flyer" (4-6 per sheet of paper) where you can write up information about your craft business – detailing the types of products you have available and give your name, address and phone number or web address where people can contact you for a catalog, or further information about what you have available. Cut the mini-flyers apart to use. These "mini-flyers" can then be put into every bill you pay (Sears, Visa, and others all have additional advertising on the outside of their billing envelopes as well as items on the inside that you can purchase, so why not put YOUR information into the return envelope when you pay your bills?). Look at it this way, the clerks who open mail all day must get pretty bored with the job, so when your "mini-flyer", printed on brightly colored paper, falls out of your payment envelope, I can assure you, it will get read, and possibly even passed around to the others that are opening mail and recording the payments. This could be regarded as FREE advertising, because you have to pay for the stamp to mail your bill anyway, you might as well get some extra mileage out of that stamp!

13 ADDITIONAL WAYS TO PROFIT FROM YOUR TALENT

ADULT EDUCATION PROGRAMS at local high schools are always looking for new classes to offer to the adults in the area. Whatever your area of skill may be, consider putting together a 6 or 8-week class to offer. To do this, simply make an outline of a topic or craft that you'd like to teach each time the class meets. Figure out what the students would need to bring to the classes, or plan your fee to include the supplies to insure that every student has all the supplies necessary. If there is an instruction sheet necessary for the students to take home with them, be sure to make enough copies so everyone will have one. The "teaching" is very simple if you just talk to the students as if they were coming to work for you to help make the item and you need to tell them how to do it.

ARTS & CRAFTS SHOPS are also always looking for people to teach classes on various subjects. These classes would be short one or two hour classes, rather than an on-going 6 or 8-week class schedule. You could perhaps teach your class once a month or quarterly, or whatever you set up with the shop owner. Fees for classes vary – some will pay a flat fee for the class while others pay so much per student that registers and attends.

WRITE AND PUBLISH your knowledge and talent in book form or reports or newsletters to get out to your customers (our book *"Write 'How-To' Books That SELL"* will get you going in this direction). With just a little help and instruction to write your information, you can literally make thousands and thousands of dollars selling your own specific information product!

SELL CRAFT PATTERNS to customers and other do-it-yourself people. Write out complete instructions on how to make some of your better selling items. There are always people who will look at your crafts and say "That's very nice – I can make those". Usually these people don't buy your product, but you can be sure most will never get around to figuring out how to make it either. So, for those folks having the pattern available could make a sale for you that you wouldn't have had otherwise.

SELL CRAFT KITS. Perhaps you might want to put your pattern and instructions AND all the supplies necessary to complete a craft item into a package and sell it to that customer who wants to make it herself. Packaged do-it-yourself craft items like this make very good sellers through mail order.

START A PARTY PLAN BUSINESS. A friend and her husband make beautiful wood items that are extremely good sellers. A few years ago they started their own party plan business and work it just like Tupperware or Mary Kay parties where the hostess gets gifts for X number of people there, X number of dollars in sales, and X number of parties scheduled from her party. They have a very good business, especially since all the profit goes to them because they are making the items that they are promoting and not paying another source.

BE A GUEST SPEAKER for various clubs and craft organizations. Prepare a talk and demonstration that will teach and inform the listeners. At the beginning you may get only $50 to $100 for your talk, but as you get more proficient and your name starts to be known, you'll be able to ask much higher fees for your speaking engagements. These talks also lead to sales so you'll have another source of income from speaking to groups.

TURN YOUR HOME INTO A MARKETPLACE during the holiday season. We know a craft lady who invites other craftspeople to show their crafts at her home during the Thanksgiving weekend every year. Each person's crafts are tagged with small tags with the price and have a separate code for each craftsperson. She and her family literally move in with her sister for the weekend as her own house has been turned into a "Show room" of assorted craft items ranging from wreaths, wood items, ceramics, dolls, fancy pillows, decorated cinnamon brooms, wall hangings, and much more! As the customers wander through the house (every bedroom, bathroom, living room, dining room laundry room and kitchen are FILLED with craft items) they can gather together the things they want to purchase, then as they go on to the kitchen area, the woman has cookies and brownies and coffee and spiced tea for the guests. The guests go on from the kitchen area out through the laundry room and into the garage where a table is set up with cash registers and the sales are written up. As the sales are written up on sales receipts, the coded price tags are removed and put into an empty margarine container to be separated later. This one weekend of work generates thousands of dollars for the crafters, and becomes bigger each year as the previous years' attendees bring their friends and family members.

INDUSTRY TRADE SHOWS offer opportunities for those who have special and unique skills. Perhaps there are major craft shows that offer "mini classes" to the participants. It would be wise to inquire about teaching one of these mini classes. Not only does this bring attention to your booth, but if you decide to sell packaged kits and patterns as well as the completed product, many of the individuals who attend your "class" will immediately follow you to your booth and table and purchase items you've been "teaching" them about in the class, as well as other items that they see while they're at your booth.

SELL YOUR ORIGINAL DESIGNS to magazines. The editors of craft, hobby and handyman magazines buy how-to projects every month, paying from $25 to $350 per design or project. Contact the editors of various magazines and tell them about your special original pattern and include a picture of the finished item. If they are interested in the pattern they will write an offer letter to you. (The down side to selling your original pattern to a craft magazine is that there will be many crafters who will fall in love with the design and begin making it themselves, and you may find your special item showing up on several tables at a craft fair where you previously would have had no competition with that particular item.)

The main thing to remember in your own business is not to give up. You may make many mistakes at the beginning, and we all have done that, you just need to learn from them and go on. The craft business is an extremely profitable business, whether you decide to work it part time or full time. Good luck in your new business venture!

14 IMPORTANT DISCLAIMER

In this book, the author and publisher have tried to get you enthused about starting your own business. We have talked about the craft business, which we believe to have good profit potential for the beginning entrepreneur. However, you must realize that the possibility of failure is a fact of life in the business world. There is no business on this earth where everybody succeeds (if there were such a business, every person in America would immediately quit their current job and go into that business).

There are many, many variables, any one of which could make your business venture show little or no profit. Your own initiative and desire will play the greatest part in whether your business will be a success. We remind you that nothing printed in this book should be interpreted as a guarantee, on the part of the author or the publisher, that your business will be profitable.

All of the information in this book reflects the opinions of the author. While we believe that the information is accurate as of the date of printing, it is possible that there are errors of omission.

This book is not intended to give legal or financial advice, since neither the author nor the publishers are accountants or attorneys. Whenever you need such advice, you must consult a professional lawyer or accountant, or both.

The "checklist for starting your craft business" is simply a guide for you to follow as you get your business up and running. The purpose of this section is to give you a "handle" on your business venture. Many times in a new business the small things are overlooked, and every detail, whether large or small is important to a profitable business.

By following this guide the new business can be started in a systematic way. This guide is a series of questions that you may answer so that you'll know at a glance what has been done and what yet needs to be done. Answer the questions in your own unique way and according to your needs now. The various subjects are listed in alphabetical order – you may re-arrange them if you wish.

15 ADVERTISING

1. Do you have a budget for advertising?

2. Have you decided which type of advertising to do first – newspaper advertising, Internet website or mailing out flyers?

3. Have you visited several printers and checked prices on printing? (Check with several and ask the same questions of each of them – how long until you'd get your finished printing, prices, will they help you choose paper colors or give suggestions to make your flyers better?) Don't forget to compare prices with online printers.

4. Have you made arrangements to have your business cards made? (This is one of the first things you need to do).

5. Have you contacted your local Post Office to get information about bulk mailing? They have packages of information already made up to give to individuals who are thinking about doing this type of mailing for advertising purposes.

6. Have you checked with craft supply stores and general merchandise stores to see if you can put a full or half page flyer on a bulletin board or wall where their customers can see it?

7.   Have you looked into getting your own domain name, web hosting, or other online presence like an eBay or Etsy store?

16 BUSINESS NAME

1. Have you avoided the trite and <u>not</u> called your business "Your Name Enterprises?"

2. Is your name selection appropriate to your business? Will potential customers know what type of business you're actually in? ("Diana's Repairs" tells the customer nothing, whereas "Diana's Doll Repair" tells the whole story!)

3. Is your name short enough that it will help cut costs in the Classified Ads that you will be placing ("Diana's Doll Repair" is certainly fewer words than "Diana's Doll Repair and Doll Repair Kits", even though you may sell repair parts for other people to purchase from you. Save that information for your flyers, newsletters and brochures.

4. Have you tried out your name on others (family, friends and business associates) before going to the printer for letterhead and business cards?

5. Will the name you select lend itself to a distinctive logo, if you choose to use a logo?

6. Have you checked to see if your name is available for registration as a domain name? (We like GoDaddy because they're inexpensive and have great customer

service)

7. Add up the cost of using your selected name for a year (ads, business cards, flyers, etc.) then consider how much it could cost you to change the name. Are you ready to live with it or risk that extra expense? Also, changing names several times is confusing to your regular customers – what is your name THIS week?

17 CLASSIFIED ADS

1. Have you written the ad out in full? (Don't worry about the word count now, but get all the benefits to the reader down on paper. Benefits include FREE delivery, demonstrations available, personalization, and other key features)

2. Does your ad contain the AIDA principle for all good advertising -- Attention, Interest, Desire and Action?

3. Did you begin your ad with a benefit to the reader?

4. Have you started your ad with the popular "pulling power" words "How to..." or with an active verb, such as "Get", "Save", "Make", etc? The most powerful word of all – "FREE" can certainly be used in this home-based business of crafting! "FREE delivery" of large orders, or "FREE delivery" to Consignment Shops, etc.

5. Are your name, address, phone number and/or web address complete and correct?

6. If you get a call tomorrow, are your crafts prepared and ready to sell or to show if someone wants you to come to a meeting and give a demonstration?

18 COMPANY

1. How have you organized your company? Have you compared the advantages and disadvantages of single proprietorship, partnership, and corporation?

2. Have you researched or talked with your accountant about the tax advantages and disadvantages of the different methods of organizing your business?

3. Have you gone to the local Internal Revenue Service, online to IRS.gov or your accountant to pick up a copy of a "Schedule C" so you can become familiar with all the various types of expenses that are allowed by the Internal Revenue Service and deductions that you can make?

4. Have you picked up a pocket size calendar that you'll need to keep in your vehicle to note mileage each day and also make a notation of where you wentyou're your deduction at the end of the year ("Mary Smith - delivered crafts" or "Post Office - mail flyers")?

5. Have you thought about some extra items you'd like to sell to your craft customers – perhaps packaged "kits" or patterns, perhaps a newsletter about crafts? Do you have an ample supply of craft items on hand when you open your doors for business? Do you have a nice variety

of items so people have several things to choose from, therefore making larger sales than if you only offer one item?

19 COMPLAINTS

1. Remember that old saying that the customer is always right? Well even when they're not, do you treat your customers as you would like to be treated?

2. Do you take care of complaints quickly? (A prompt response can be more than half of the solution to the complaint.) If there was a defective part on your craft item, that you didn't know was there and the customer discovered it when she got home, your response should always be an apology along with a new item. If you try to avoid the caller, the problem gets bigger and bigger until the dissatisfied customer begins complaining to all her friends. Even if you have to lose money on "making it right" with the customer, you'll be the winner in the end.

20 CUSTOMER PAYMENT

1. Are you aware of the problems that could arise if you go with a "Bill Me" payment method?   We NEVER bill customers for purchases – we deal strictly on a "cash and carry" type of business.   We also discourage COD shipments if you're doing business by mail.   It has been our experience, and other professional mail order entrepreneurs will say, that nearly 75% of people who order COD will change their mind when the shipment gets to them, in which case you'll be stuck with the additional COD charges and no sale at all.   We believe that those who really want the item will either send you a check or money order or will charge it on one of their charge cards.

2. Do you accept checks? We've found that very few checks bounce, but if you're not sure on new customers, you can always go straight to the customer's bank and cash it immediately instead of running it through your own bank.   Additionally, be sure to collect additional identification information such as a driver's license number and work phone number when accepting checks from customers you don't know.

3. Do you offer credit card service? This is not a "must" and will not slow down your business. However,

in some instances, if you are selling higher ticket items, or if someone wants to purchase a large amount of craft items they may ask if you take either Visa or MasterCard. At the beginning we would advise you to just stick with cash and checks for the crafts that you sell. (you can get a merchant account through your local bank or online through services like those provided by Electronic Transfer, Inc. or goEmerchant). We also highly recommend PayPal and Square as both have small portable credit card readers that you can use by attaching to your smartphone.

21 DISPLAY ADVERTISING

1. Does your ad use a simple headline that promises an immediate benefit to the reader?

2. Is your copy (wording within the display ad) lively and oriented to the reader?

3. Does your ad tell why your products are unique and why the customer should give you a call?

4. Have you given the price? Are you going to give them a "Special Price" or a "coupon" that gives a discount off the regular price or discount for purchasing several items?

5. Have you listed the customer benefits? (Items are "One of a kind", personalized, custom, etc.)

6. Have you ended your ad with your company name, address and phone number or web address? How can anyone contact you if you forget to put your phone number in the ad? Different customers will prefer different methods of contacting you so be sure to provide as many as you possibly can.

22 PRICING

1. How do you arrive at the price for your crafts?

2. Are you familiar with the competition's pricing? Have you checked around to see what the "retail establishments" and other crafters are charging?

3. Are you familiar enough with the psychology of pricing that you know that a cut-rate price does not always mean a jump in sales? (After all, you're offering benefits that the "retail establishments" cannot offer -- quality handmade items, one-of-a-kind items, etc.)

23 RECORDS

1. Have you set up a system for keeping full and accurate records of your customers? Have you purchased a card file or created a computer database to indicate dates of purchase of each of your customers so you'll be able to send out additional flyers and catalogs to them?

2. Do you have a record of the results of your mailings of flyers -- how many people responded and how many craft items did you sell?

3. Are you keeping track of the classified ads?

4. If you've placed your business in the yellow pages of the phone book (and we highly recommend that you do since that's the first place someone would look when they are looking for your type of product or service), are you making a note on the customer record card that he or she got your name from the phone book?

5. Do you know the months that are best for major advertisements of your business? (such as Mother's Day, Valentine's Day, and Christmas).

24 REFERRALS

1. Do you ask your customers to refer you to their friends and co-workers? Have you given them business cards to pass out?

2. Do you suggest additional purchases when you are making the sale of the initial item? If you don't mention other things available, the customer may not be aware of what else you have.

25 IN A NUTSHELL

- Be sure to read this instruction manual from front to back at least once. If you aren't completely sure of what to do or where to begin, read the manual again. Don't try to jump into a business too quickly and ignore the directions and instructions we've mapped out.

- NEVER use "grocery" or "rent" money to begin ANY business. There is no business that can guarantee success, much less "overnight" riches. If you don't have enough money to at least get a booth at a local mall craft show, we suggest you save amounts of money each week until you do have enough to start.

- Never take in a partner (if short of cash yourself) in this business (except your spouse). No two people think alike and you'll be headed for trouble if you look for an outside partner in this type of business.

- Because you are the boss of your business, it will be up to you to motivate yourself to do the necessary work to remain in business (our book *"501 Tips, Strategies and Professional Secrets for Home Business Entrepreneurs"* will give many ideas and tips to keep you in business, and the book *"Complete Guide to Home Business Riches - 25 confidential reports"* will help to organize your "home office", help in advertising, help to get and keep customers, and much more).

- Be sure to have an ample supply of craft items available when you open your doors for business, otherwise you could be bought out in a day or two, leaving you without a business at all.

- If you intend to do business by mail order, use small classified ads to advertise your catalog of products or to invite inquiries about a certain item you have available. Never jump into a mail order business with expensive display ads, when the same amount of money could have been used to place 5, 10 or 20 classified ads in an assortment of magazines.

- Never ask for $1 "shipping and handling" or "SASE" or "2 first class stamps" when advertising your FREE catalog. Let your FREE information BE free!

- Be sure your printing and copying is professional looking and not "copies of copies of copies" that are so faded they are hardly readable. Quality flyers sent out will result in a much better return in quantity of orders!

- Pay special attention to the packaging of your items. Make your items as appealing as possible, and professional looking.

- You MUST follow the advice on keeping records of each advertisement that you place, as well as all the orders you receive from craft shows, etc., in order to track the profit from each venture.

- Avoid immediate consumerism. Put your money back into your business to make it grow.

- Work as hard for yourself as you would for someone else. You are your own boss.

- Identify goals annually and plan accordingly. Break down the goals into monthly and weekly and daily goals.

- Look at yourself and your display often, if attending craft shows. Keep things tidy.

- Your success will come in cans, not in cannots.

- Make up your mind to stick with your new business for at least 1 to 2 years. Most people "give up" just before the success would have come. Don't plan on instant success or huge profits within the first few months. It does take time for your name to become known and to build up a customer list. After a period of time referrals will start coming, previous customers will return to buy more of your crafts, and new business will grow bigger and bigger.

Remember that, in the crafts business, you make what you make! Unique products will get your business started, and quality work will keep you in business.

ABOUT THE AUTHOR

S. Denise Hoyle learned much about Sewing and pattern design from her mother while growing up. She started her own business in high school and made extra money sewing for people and doing alterations from home for other businesses like local dry cleaners. Denise later also became interested in creating patterns and has since authored a number of specialty sewing and craft books.

While sewing is Denise's first love, the world of electronic commerce also fascinates her, and that interest led her to pursue a Masters Degree in eBusiness and Technology. Now Denise spends her time teaching business subjects to online college students, in addition to sharing her love of sewing with others through classes, instructional books, and unique pattern designs.